THE COMPLETE
CANNING COOKBOOK

By Hill Hjem

Homemade Canning Recipes
Including Jams, Jelly, Pickles, And Preserves

HILL   HJEM

ISBN:978-1-962472-17-3

Written & designed by: Rianna M. Hill

www.HillHjem.com

Hill Hjem is a Brand of Little Red Hills LLC ©2023

from Little Red Hills

WHY CAN?
The History of Canning

Welcome to the art of canning, a practice deeply rooted in history and tradition. The act of canning isn't merely about preserving food; it's a testament to human ingenuity, innovation, and the unwavering spirit to secure sustenance beyond the harvest season. Join us as we embark on a journey through time, exploring the evolution of canning and how this timeless method has shaped our culinary world.

Preserving History: A Journey Through the Evolution of Canning

Welcome to a historical voyage through the fascinating evolution of canning, an ingenious method that has revolutionized food preservation and forever altered the way we nourish ourselves.

In the Beginning

The roots of canning can be traced back to ancient civilizations, where the necessity to store food for extended periods drove early humans to develop innovative preservation techniques. While these ancient methods varied—from using honey to preserve fruits to fermentation and drying—none provided a foolproof solution for long-term storage.

The Birth of Canning

The late 18th century marked a turning point with the advent of modern canning. The visionary French confectioner, Nicolas Appert, is widely credited as the pioneer who unlocked the secret to preserving food in airtight containers. In 1809, Appert's breakthrough, based on experimentation with glass jars sealed with cork and wax, won him a cash prize from Napoleon Bonaparte, affirming the significance of his invention.

The Tin Can Revolution

Shortly after Appert's groundbreaking discovery, the Englishman Peter Durand received a patent in 1810 for preserving food in tin-plated cans, opening new possibilities for long-term food storage. This innovation swiftly gained popularity, especially among sailors and explorers, transforming the way provisions were packed for long sea voyages and expeditions.

Throughout the 19th and 20th centuries, canning continued to evolve. The method saw numerous improvements in technology and equipment, including the development of the double-seam process by American inventor John Mason, leading to the iconic Mason jar.

Canning Today

Fast forward to the present, and canning remains a cornerstone of food preservation. From traditional family recipes to innovative culinary creations, canning has transcended mere preservation to become an art form—an avenue for capturing the essence of seasonal produce and preserving it for future enjoyment.

As we delve into the recipes within these pages, we pay homage to this rich heritage. The history of canning is not just a narrative of preserving food; it's a testament to human innovation, adaptability, and the unending quest to savor the flavors of each season, year-round.

HOW TO:
getting Started with Canning

Embarking on the journey of canning holds numerous benefits. Preserving seasonal fruits, vegetables, and homemade recipes enables you to:

- Enjoy Seasonal Produce Year-round: Capture the flavors of summer to relish during winter and savor the freshness of each season.
- Ensure Quality and Control: Know precisely what goes into your canned goods, controlling the ingredients and avoiding preservatives commonly found in store-bought items.
- Cost-Effective: Buying produce in bulk during peak seasons and preserving it through canning can save money in the long run.
- Create Thoughtful Gifts: Homemade canned goods make heartfelt gifts for friends and family, showcasing your culinary prowess and care.

What to Consider Before Starting

Before diving into the canning process, consider these essential points:

- Equipment: Invest in quality canning equipment like jars, lids, canners, and utensils. The Hill Hjem canning kit is an excellent choice, offering what you need to begin your canning journey. This canning companion is a 9-in-1 kit to help you get started!
- Recipes and Resources: Gather trusted canning recipes and reliable resources (such as canning guides and books) to ensure safe and successful preservation, like this book!
- Safety First: Familiarize yourself with proper canning techniques, including sterilization, processing times, and altitude adjustments for your location.
- Storage and Labeling: Plan for adequate storage space for your canned goods and label jars with the date and contents for easy identification.

Embarking on your canning journey with the Hill Hjem canning kit is an exciting step toward culinary creativity and sustainable living. You're not just preserving food; you're preserving memories, flavors, and traditions.

With each jar you seal, you're capturing a moment in time, creating homemade delights that will bring joy and nourishment to you and your loved ones.

Remember, every jar tells a story. Start yours today with the Hill Hjem canning kit, and let your canning adventures begin!

Table of Contents

PICKLE RECIPES

MIXED VEGETABLE PICKLES

Prep time: 30 min
Cook time: 15 min

Serving: 4 pint jars

INGREDIENTS:

- 2 heads of cauliflower
- 1-2 lbs baby carrots
- 1 packet of celery ribs
- 2 lbs Broccoli
- 1 to 2 onions, peeled, sliced, and separated

Brine:

- 8 cups of vinegar
- 1 cup of pickling salt
- 8 cups of hot water

Per pint jar:

- ¼ tsp black peppercorns
- ¼ tsp mustard seeds, you can skip it if desired
- 1 to 2 garlic cloves, peeled and cut in half
- ½ to 1 tsp dill seed, you can skip it if desired

NUTRITION

Calories 45, Protein 1g, Carbohydrate 9g, Fiber 1g, Sugar 2g

DIRECTIONS:

- Firstly, rinse all vegetables under running water. Cut broccoli and cauliflower into florets. Cut celery into pieces about 1-inch.
- Place all sliced vegetables into the big bowl and combine well.
- Fill water into the big pot and place it on medium-high heat. Bring to a boil.
- To prepare the brine: Take another pot; add salt, water, and vinegar and bring to a boil. Stir well.
- Arrange prepared vegetables into the jars and pack them tightly as you can.
- When the brine gets to boil, pour the brine into the jars, leaving some space.
- Clean the edges of the jars with a kitchen towel and top each jar with a new sterilized lid.
- Place jars of pickles into the water bath canner. Let process for 15 minutes. After 15 minutes, remove them carefully and allow them to cool overnight. The next day, check the jars and make sure that all jars achieved a proper seal.
- Allow the jars to leave for a few days. You can store them in a dark and cool place for up to one year.

PICKLED SWEET MUSTARD

Prep time: 15 min
Cook time: 40 min
Process time: 15 min

Serving: 8 pint jars

INGREDIENTS:

- 1 head of cauliflower
- 3 lbs pickling cucumbers
- 6 cups of white vinegar
- 1 lb pearl onions
- 3 cups of water
- 2 tbsp pickling salt
- 3 ½ cups granulated sugar
- 1 tbsp turmeric powder
- 6 tbsp mustard powder
- 2/3 cup of clear Jel
- 2 tbsp pickling spice

NUTRITION

Calories 645, Protein 5g,
Carbohydrate 153g, Fiber
5g, Sugar 132g

DIRECTIONS:

- Firstly, rinse all vegetables under clean water.
- Cut cauliflower into florets. Peel pearl onion and sliced cucumber into thick slices. Add water into the big pot. Place it over medium-high heat. Bring to a boil.
- Add turmeric, mustard powder, salt, sugar, water, and vinegar to another pot. Bring to a boil. Stir well.
- Cut two squares from the cheesecloth, place pickling spice in the middle of the cheesecloth, close the edges of the cloth to enclose the spices, and tie the packet with the twine.
- When the brine comes to a boil, add a spice packet and boil for 10 to 15 minutes. Remove the spice packet and then add vegetables and stir well. Bring to a boil for 10 minutes.
- Take little brine and mix with clear jel until smooth. Add it back to the pot and stir well. Let boil for 5 minutes more. Turn off the heat. Place pickles into the jars and leave a little spice.
- Clean the edges of the jars with a kitchen towel and top each jar with a new sterilized lid. Place jars of pickles into the water bath canner. Let process for 15 minutes.
- Remove them and let them cool overnight. The next day, check the jars and make sure that all jars achieved a proper seal.
- Allow the jars to leave for a few days. You can store them in a dark and cool place for up to one year.

PICKLED BRUSSELS SPROUTS

Prep time: 30 min
Cook time: 10 min

Serving: 6 pint jars

INGREDIENTS:

- 3 lbs Brussels sprouts, trimmed and halved
- 6 garlic cloves, halved
- 2 tsp red pepper flakes, crushed
- 2 ½ cups of white vinegar
- 2 ½ cups of water
- Sweet red pepper, 1, chopped
- 1 onion, chopped
- 3 tbsp canning salt
- 1 tbsp celery seed
- ½ cup sugar
- 1 tbsp whole peppercorns

DIRECTIONS:

- Add water to the Dutch oven and bring to a boil. Then, add Brussels sprouts and cook for 4 minutes until tender. Remove with a slotted spoon. Then, transfer it into the ice water. Let drain and pat dry them.
- Place Brussels sprouts into the six jars. Top with pepper flakes and garlic.
- Add the remaining ingredients into the saucepan and bring to a boil. Add this liquid over Brussels sprouts and remove air bubbles from the jars. Wipe rims and place lids on jars. Apply bands.
- Prepare the water bath canner. Add water to the water bath canning. Bring to a boil. Place sterilized jars into the water bath canner.
- Let process for 10 minutes. After 10 minutes, remove jars from the water bath canner. Let cool it.

NUTRITION

Calories 17, Protein 1g, Carbohydrate 3g, Fat 0g, Sugar 1g

PICKLED SWEET PEPPERS

Prep time: 30 min
Cook time: 15 min

Serving: 5 pint jars

INGREDIENTS:

- 5 sweet red peppers
- 1 onion, thinly sliced
- 4 tsp canola oil
- 8 banana peppers
- 8 garlic cloves, peeled
- 1 ¼ cups of sugar
- 2 ½ cups of white vinegar
- 2 tsp canning salt
- 2 ½ cups of water

DIRECTIONS:

- Firstly, slice red and banana peppers into strips. Remove seeds. Place peppers into five 1-pint jars. Top with garlic, canola oil, and onion.
- Add sugar, salt, vinegar, and water into the saucepan and boil. Place hot liquid over the pepper mixture. Remove any air bubbles from the jars. Wipe the rims and place the lid on the jars. Apply band.
- Prepare the water bath canner. Add water to the water bath canning. Bring to a boil. Place sterilized jars into the water bath canner.
- Let process for 15 minutes. After 15 minutes, remove jars from the water bath canner. Let cool it.

NUTRITION

Calories 728, Protein 3g,
Carbohydrate 171g, Fat 1g,
Sugar 162g

SPICY PICKLED GARLIC

Prep time: 20 min
Cook time: 10 min

Serving: 3 pint jars

INGREDIENTS:

- 1 ½ cups white wine vinegar
- 2 quarts water
- 3 cups garlic cloves, peeled
- 6 whole peppercorns
- 12 coriander seeds
- 3 whole allspice
- 1 bay leaf, torn into 3 pieces
- 3 dried hot chilies, split
- 1 tbsp sugar
- 1 ½ tsp canning salt

DIRECTIONS:

- Add water to the saucepan and bring to a boil. Then, add garlic and boil for 1 minute.
- Add bay leaf, allspice, chilies, peppercorns, and coriander among three jars. Drain the garlic and place it into the jars.
- Add salt, sugar, and vinegar into the saucepan and boil.
- Pour hot liquid over garlic. Remove any air bubbles. Wipe the rim and place lids on the jars.
- Prepare the water bath canner. Add water to the water bath canning. Bring to a boil. Place sterilized jars into the water bath canner.
- Let process for 10 minutes. After 10 minutes, remove jars from the water bath canner. Let cool it.

NUTRITION

Calories 33, Protein 1g, Carbohydrate 6g, Fat 0g, Sugar 1g

SWEET AND SPICY PICKLE RELISH

Prep time: 20 min
Cook time: 45 min

Serving: 5 pint jars

INGREDIENTS:

- 3 cups green pepper, grated
- 3 cups pickling cucumber, grated
- 1 cup onion, minced or grated
- 2 cups apple cider vinegar
- 1 cup granulated sugar
- 1 tbsp kosher salt
- 1 tbsp mustard seed
- ½ tsp celery seed
- 1 tsp red chili flakes

DIRECTIONS:

- Add onion, cucumber, and green pepper to the pot. Add 1 cup of apple cider vinegar and simmer for 30 minutes. Drain the vegetables and discard the liquid. Add the vegetables back to the pot.
- Add remaining vinegar, spices, and sugar and simmer for 5 minutes. Remove the pot from the heat.
- Fill the jars, wipe the rims, and apply lids and rings.
- Process the jars into the water bath canner for 10 minutes.
- Remove the jars from the pot.
- When done, store it in a cool place for up to 1 year.

NUTRITION

Calories 707, Protein 11g, Carbohydrate 104g, Fat 26g, Sugar 1g

PICKLED SUGAR PUMPKIN

 Prep time: 5 min
Cook time: 1 hr

 Serving: 2 pint jars

INGREDIENTS:

- 8 cups sugar pumpkin, cubed
- 3 cups apple cider vinegar
- 2 cups water
- 2 cups granulated white sugar
- 20 black peppercorns
- 15 whole cloves
- 10 allspice berries
- 2 sticks cinnamon, crushed
- 1 bay leaf

DIRECTIONS:

- Prepare the boiling water bath canner. Add lids into the saucepan and simmer it over low heat.
- Add sugar, water, and vinegar into the saucepan and heat it.
- Add bay leaf, cinnamon stick, allspice berries, cloves, and peppercorn into the spice bag. Add pumpkin and spice bag and boil it. Then, lower the heat and simmer it.
- Cook pumpkin in brine for 30 to 40 minutes.
- When done, add it to the jar. Cover with brine and leave ½-inch space. Process it in the boiling water bath canner for 20 minutes.
- When time is up, remove jars from the canner.
- Allow it to cool.
- Store it.

NUTRITION

Calories 83, Protein 0g, Carbohydrate 20g, Fat 0g, Sugar 18g

PICKLED ZUCCHINI

Prep time: 30 min
Cook time: 5 min

Serving: 20

INGREDIENTS:

- 2 lbs zucchini, thinly sliced
- ½ lb onions, quartered and thinly sliced
- ¼ cup salt
- 2 cups white sugar
- 2 cups apple cider vinegar
- 1 tsp celery seed
- 1 tsp ground turmeric
- 1 tsp yellow mustard
- 2 tsp mustard seeds

DIRECTIONS:

- Add onions and zucchini into the bowl and cover with water. Then, add salt and stir well. Soak it for 2 hours. Then, drain it.
- Transfer it to the bowl.
- Add mustard seeds, mustard, turmeric, celery seed, vinegar, and sugar into the saucepan and boil it. Add this mixture over zucchini and onion and allow it to stand for 2 hours.
- Add pickling liquid, spices, onion, and zucchini back to the pot and boil it for 3 minutes.
- Meanwhile, add water to the pot and boil it for 5 minutes. Add jars and simmer them.
- Pack the jars with a pickling mixture.
- Remove any air bubbles, leave a ¼-inch space, and place the lid on the jars.
- Add water into the pot and boil it. Add jars to it and boil it.
- Process for 10 minutes.
- Remove the jars from the canner.
- Store it in a cool and dark area overnight.

NUTRITION

Calories 8, Protein 0g,
Carbohydrate 0g, Fat 0g,
Sugar 0g

PICKLED MUSHROOMS

 Prep time: 30 min
Cook time: 20 min

 Serving: 12

INGREDIENTS:

- 2 lbs mushrooms
- 5 garlic cloves
- ½ cup white vinegar, 5% acidity
- 2 cups water
- 1 tbsp sugar
- 1 tbsp salt
- 6 bay leaves
- 8 whole peppercorns
- 6 tbsp vinegar

NUTRITION

Calories 26, Protein 2g,
Carbohydrate 4g, Fat 1g,
Sugar 3g

DIRECTIONS:

- Clean and rinse mushrooms and add them to the pot. Fill enough water to cover the mushrooms.
- Add ½ cup of white vinegar to the water and boil it. Cook for 15 minutes.
- When mushrooms are cooked, drain the liquid and keep it aside.
- Add peppercorns, bay leaves, salt, and water to another pot and boil it. Add 6 tbsp of vinegar and stir well. Then, remove it from heat and keep it aside.
- Clean and dice the garlic into small pieces. Then, add it to the bottom of the jars. Fill the jars with cooked mushrooms.
- Pour marinade over the mushrooms. Remove any air bubbles.
- Wipe the rims and apply the lids and rings.
- They can be stored in the refrigerator for up to several weeks.

PICKLED RED ONIONS

Prep time: 5 min
Cook time: 30 min

Serving: 2 cups

INGREDIENTS:

- 1 red onion, peeled and very thinly sliced
- 3/4 cup apple cider vinegar
- 1/4 cup water
- 1 tsp fine sea salt
- 1-2 tbsp sweetener

DIRECTIONS:

- Add salt, sweetener, water, and vinegar to the saucepan and cook over medium-high heat.
- Add thinly sliced to the Mason jar. Pour the hot vinegar mixture over the onions and screw on the lid. Shake the onion until they are coated with the vinegar mixture.
- Allow the onions to marinate for 30 seconds.
- Place it into the fridge in a sealed container for up to 2 weeks.

NUTRITION

Calories 14, Protein 1g,
Carbohydrate 3g, Fat 1g,
Sugar 2g

PICKLED JALAPEÑOS

Prep time: 5 min
Cook time: 5 min

Serving: 10

INGREDIENTS:

- 8 jalapenos
- 5 Garlic cloves, chopped
- 1 cup water
- 1 cup white wine vinegar
- 1 tbsp peppercorns
- 1 tbsp salt
- 2 tbsp sugar

DIRECTIONS:

- Cut the jalapenos into thin rings without removing any of the seeds.
- Add peppercorns, salt, sugar, water, and vinegar to the pot and boil it. Keep it aside.
- Use tongs to transfer the jalapenos and garlic into a clean jar. Ladle the pickling juices until you've reached the top of the jar. Let cool at room temperature before securing a lid and popping them into the fridge.

NUTRITION

Calories 340, Protein 3g,
Carbohydrate 70g, Fat 1g,
Sugar 62g

PICKLED TOMATOES

Prep time: 5 min
Cook time: 30 min

Serving: 10

INGREDIENTS:

- 3 lbs roma tomatoes, washed and dried
- 4 garlic cloves, sliced
- 4 bay leaves
- 1 bunch parsley
- 1 bunch dill, 3-4 stems
- 1 stalk scallions
- 3 oak leaves
- 2 tbsp whole black peppercorns
- 6 tbsp sea salt
- 2 tbsp sugar
- 2 tbsp white wine vinegar

DIRECTIONS:

- Sterilize jars and lids in boiling water in a large pot for 15 minutes. Remove them from the water with cooking tongs.
- Add oat leaves, scallions, dill, parsley, bay leaves, garlic, and tomatoes to the jars. Fill the jars with boiling water.
- Prepare the brine: Pour the water from the jars into a pot. Add sugar, salt, and black peppercorns and boil for 5 minutes. Then, add vinegar and stir well.
- Pour the brine back into the jars. Add more boiling water and remove any space before you put the lid on to prevent leaking. Close the lids.
- Turn the jars upside down for two to three days.
- Pickled tomatoes are ready within one or two weeks, depending on the size. Store them at room temperature or lower before opening.

NUTRITION

Calories 31, Protein 2g,
Carbohydrate 7g, Fat 1g,
Sugar 4g

WATERMELON RIND PICKLES

Prep time: 10 hrs
Cook time: 25 min

Serving: 5

INGREDIENTS:

- 2 lbs watermelon rind
- 1 cup apple cider vinegar
- 1 cup water
- ¾ cup sugar
- ¼ cup ginger, chopped
- 4 tsp kosher salt
- 1 tsp red pepper flake
- 1 tsp allspice berries
- 1 star anise pod

DIRECTIONS:

- Remove and discard the exterior green portion of the watermelon rind with a sharp peeler. Cut into 1-inch cubes.
- Add spices, salt, ginger, sugar, water, and apple cider vinegar to the saucepan and place it over medium-high heat. Boil for 1 minute. Add watermelon and return to a boil. Turn off the heat. Remove the pan from the heat and allow it to cool for 30 minutes.
- Move the pickles to a 2-quart jar using a canning funnel and ladle. Pour on as much of the pickling juice as possible. Cover the jar and leave it at room temperature for another 1 1/2 hours.
- Refrigerate overnight and consume within a month. These pickles must be refrigerated.

NUTRITION

Calories 212, Protein 1g,
Carbohydrate 55g, Fat 0g,
Sugar 48g

PICKLED GREEN BEANS

Prep time: 10 min
Cook time: 10 min

Serving: 8

INGREDIENTS:

- 1 lb green beans
- 2 tbsp thyme
- 2 garlic cloves, sliced thinly
- ½ tsp red pepper flakes
- 2 cups water
- 1 cup vinegar
- 1 tbsp salt
- 1 tbsp sugar

DIRECTIONS:

- Rinse green beans and remove the stems.
- Add sliced green beans, red pepper flakes, garlic, and thyme to the jar.
- Add sugar, salt, water, and vinegar to the saucepan and boil it. When boiled, pour into the jar until the liquid completely submerges the green beans. Close the lid on the jar and remove any air bubbles.
- Allow the jar cool on the counter until it reaches room temperature.
- When cooled, place the jar into the fridge and allow it to pickle for 3 hours.
- Quick pickled green beans are good for up to one month in the refrigerator.

NUTRITION

Calories 32, Protein 1g,
Carbohydrate 6g, Fat 1g,
Sugar 3g

DILL PICKLED RADISHES

Prep time: 10 min
Cook time: 10 min

Serving: 8

INGREDIENTS:

- 1lb radishes
- ¾ cup dill
- 2 tbsp mustard seeds
- 2 cloves garlic, sliced thinly
- ¼ tsp red pepper flakes
- 2 cups water
- 1 cup vinegar
- 1 tbsp salt
- 1 tbsp sugar

NUTRITION

Calories 26, Protein 1g,
Carbohydrate 5g, Fat 1g,
Sugar 2g

DIRECTIONS:

- Cut the radish root from the leaves and rinse well to remove excess dirt. Cut them into thin slices.
- Add sliced radish, red pepper flakes, garlic, mustard seeds, and dill to the jar.
- Add sugar, vinegar, salt, and water to the saucepan and boil it.
- When boiled, pour into the jar until the liquid completely submerges the radishes. Close the lid and remove any bubbles.
- Once cooled, put the jar into the refrigerator and let the radishes pickle for at least 4 hours before serving, but for best results, serve after at least 24 hours. Quick pickled radishes are good for up to 2-3 months in the refrigerator.

PICKLED GRAPES

Prep time: 10 min
Cook time: 10 min

Serving: 12

INGREDIENTS:

- 1lb grapes
- 2-inch ginger root
- 2 sticks cinnamon
- 2 tbsp mustard seeds
- 2 cups water
- 1 cup red wine vinegar
- 1 cup apple cider vinegar
- 1 tbsp salt
- ½ cup sugar

DIRECTIONS:

- Remove grapes from the stem and rinse under clean water.
- Add mustard seeds, cinnamon sticks, ginger, and grapes to the jar.
- Add sugar, salt, apple cider vinegar, red wine vinegar, and water to the saucepan. When boiling, pour into the jar until the liquid completely submerges the grapes. Close the lid.
- Let the jar cool on the counter until it reaches room temperature. Once cooled, put the jar into the refrigerator and let the grapes pickle for at least 2 hours before serving, but for best results, serve after at least 24 hours. Pickled grapes are good for up to one month in the refrigerator.

NUTRITION

Calories 82, Protein 1g,
Carbohydrate 18g, Fat 1g,
Sugar 16g

PICKLED PEPPERS

Prep time: 10 min
Cook time: 10 min

Serving: 1 quart

INGREDIENTS:

- 1 tbsp olive oil
- 4 cups chilies
- 4 garlic cloves, sliced in half
- 1 ¾ cups white vinegar
- ¾ cup water
- 1 tbsp sugar
- ½ tsp salt
- 1 bay leaf
- 1-2 tsp whole coriander seed
- 1-2 tsp cloves
- 1-2 tsp peppercorns
- 1-2 tsp whole cumin seed
- 1-2 tsp whole mustard seed

DIRECTIONS:

- Add olive oil to the skillet and heat it over medium-high.
- Add garlic and chilies and sauté for 5 minutes until softened.
- Add garlic and chilies to the sanitized jar.
- Add salt, sugar, water, and vinegar to the saucepan and heat it.
- Pour the vinegar mixture over chilies mixture and allow the content of the jar to cool at room temperature.
- Seal the jar and refrigerate.
- Pickled peppers will stay fresh in an air-tight jar for up to 1 month.

NUTRITION

Calories 18, Protein 0.2g,
Carbohydrate 3.7g, Fat
0.1g, Sugar 3.1g

PICKLED PEARS

Prep time: 5 min
Cook time: 10 min

Serving: 4

INGREDIENTS:

- 2 pears
- 1 tsp vanilla extract
- 1 stick cinnamon
- 2 star anise
- 2 cups water
- 1 cup apple cider vinegar
- 1 tsp salt
- 1 tbsp maple syrup

DIRECTIONS:

- Rinse pears and remove the stems. Then turn each pear on its side, cut it into round slices, core and all, and remove the seeds.
- Add cinnamon sticks, star anise, vanilla extract, and pear slices to the jar and stir well.
- Add maple syrup, salt, apple cider vinegar, and water to the saucepan and boil until the sugar is dissolved. Add brine to the jar with the pears.
- When cooled, place the jars into the refrigerator and allow them to pickle for 2 hours.
- Pickled pears are good for up to two weeks in the refrigerator.

NUTRITION

Calories 496, Protein 16.6g, Carbohydrate 50.2g, Fat 26.9g, Sugar 0g

JELLIES
RECIPES

MANDARIN ORANGE JELLY

Prep time: 45 min
Cook time: 20 min

Serving: 20

INGREDIENTS:

- 4 cups mandarin juice
- 7 cups sugar
- ¼ cup lemon juice
- 1 tbsp butter
- 1 packet pectin

DIRECTIONS:

- Sterilize the jars, lids, and rings.
- Prepare the juice of lemons and mandarins.
- Add butter, sugar, and orange juice to the pan and place it over high heat. Boil for 1 minute.
- Add pectin and boil it for 1 minute.
- Remove from the heat. Add hot jelly into the sterilized jar.
- Wipe off the tops of the jars and place the lid on.
- Process it in a hot water bath for 10 minutes.
- Store it.

NUTRITION

Calories 996, Protein 1g,
Carbohydrate 251g, Fat 2g,
Sugar 246g

MINT JELLY

Prep time: 20 min
Cook time: 40 min

Serving: 4 1/2 pint jar

INGREDIENTS:

- 2 tbsp lemon juice
- 1 ½ cups mint, leaves and stems
- 1 drop green food color
- 2 ¼ cups boiling water
- 3 ½ cups white sugar
- 6 oz liquid pectin

DIRECTIONS:

- Rinse mint leaves and stems and put them into the saucepan.
- Then, crush the mint leaves with a potato masher.
- Add water to the saucepan and bring to a boil.
- Remove from the heat and cover the saucepan. Let stand for 10 minutes. Strain it.
- Add 1 2/3 cups of mint into the saucepan. Add food color and lemon juice and stir well. Add sugar and mix it well on high heat. Bring to a boil. Stir well. When boiled, add pectin and stir well.
- Remove from the heat. After that, for five minutes, sterilize the jars and lids in the boiled water. Place jelly into the hot and sterilized jars and wipe the rims with a paper towel. Place lids tightly.
- Add water into the water bath canner and boil on a high heat.
- Place jars into the water bath canner and bring to a boil. Cover the water bath canner and process for 10 minutes.

NUTRITION

Calories 61, Protein 0g,
Carbohydrate 15g, Fat 0g,
Sugar 14g

RHUBARB JELLY

Prep time: 20 min
Cook time: 10 min

Serving: 8 1/2 pint jar

INGREDIENTS:

- 4-5lbs rhubarb, cut into pieces
- 7 cups sugar
- 1-2 drops of red food coloring
- 6 oz liquid fruit pectin

DIRECTIONS:

- Add rhubarb into the food processor and grind it.
- Place cheesecloth over the bowl and add rhubarb into the strainer. Cover the edges of the cheesecloth. Let stand for a half-hour.
- Add juice to the Dutch oven. Then, add sugar and food coloring and boil on a high heat. Stir constantly.
- Add pectin and bring to a boil and stir well.
- Remove from the heat. Let stand for a few minutes.
- Place the hot mixture into hot and sterilized jars. Remove any air bubbles. Wipe rims. Place lids on the jars.
- Add water into the water bath canner and boil on a high heat.
- Place jars into the water bath canner and bring to a boil. Cover the water bath canner and process for 10 minutes.
- Let cool it.

NUTRITION

Calories 57, Protein 0g,
Carbohydrate 14g, Fat 0g,
Sugar 13g

STRAWBERRY JELLY

Prep time: 45 min
Cook time: 20 min

Serving: 20

INGREDIENTS:

- 4 cups strawberry Juice
- 1-2 tbsp lemon juice
- 1 packet powdered fruit pectin
- 1 tsp sugar

DIRECTIONS:

- Rinse and hull the strawberries.
- Add them into the saucepan with a splash of water and lemon juice.
- Mash it with a potato masher and simmer for 10 minutes.
- Strain the strawberry pulp through a jelly bag for 2 hours.
- Add this mixture to the pot and boil it. Add powdered pectin and boil it again. Add sugar and boil it again.
- Boil hard for 1 minute, and then pour this mixture into the jars.
- Process it for 10 minutes. Store it in the fridge.

NUTRITION

Calories 165, Protein 0.4g, Carbohydrate 40.7g, Fat 0.9g, Sugar 38.9g

SUN-DRIED TOMATO JELLY

Prep time: 2 hrs
Process time: 10 min

Serving: 5 1/2 jars

INGREDIENTS:

- 7 cups plum tomatoes, sliced
- 10 sun-dried tomatoes cut in half
- 2 dried hot chili peppers
- ¼ cup dry basil
- 1/3 cup balsamic vinegar
- ½ cup lemon juice
- 5 cups granulated sugar
- 170 ml liquid pectin

DIRECTIONS:

- Rinse, core, and slice tomatoes. Place it into the saucepan. Then, add sun-dried tomatoes, vinegar, basil, and chilies. Cover the pot and bring it to a boil. Lower the heat and boil for 30 minutes.
- Let chop the mixture and cool for 15 minutes.
- Place the mixture into the cheese cloth or bag.
- Add water into the water bath canner and place jars in the boiled water. But do not boil it. Place lids over it.
- Place jelly into the hot and sterilized jars.
- Remove any air bubbles. Wipe the rim of each jar. Place jars in the canner. Process it for 10 minutes.

NUTRITION

Calories 55, Protein 1g,
Carbohydrate 6g, Fat 3g,
Sugar 1g

POMEGRANATE JELLY

Prep time: 10 min
Cook time: 10 min

Serving: 20

INGREDIENTS:

- 3 1/2 cups pomegranate juice
- 4 cups sugar
- 1/4 cup lemon juice
- 1 oz pectin

DIRECTIONS:

- Break apart the pomegranates and remove the peel and white membranes. Add arils into the saucepan with ½ cup of water. Boil it. Mash the fruit to release the juice. Strain through cheesecloth.
- Add pomegranate juice into the pan with lemon juice and pectin and boil for 1 minute.
- Add sugar and stir well. Boil it for 1 minute.
- Turn off the heat.
- Add jelly into the jars.
- Remove any air bubbles. Place the lids on.
- Prepare the water bath canner: Process the jars for 10 minutes.
- Store it in the fridge for 12 to 18 months.

NUTRITION

Calories 176, Protein 0g,
Carbohydrate 11g, Fat 0g,
Sugar 10g

BLACKBERRY JELLY

 Prep time: 1 hr
Cook time: 10 min

 Serving: 20

INGREDIENTS:

- 4 cups berry juice
- 3 cups sugar

DIRECTIONS:

- Add blackberries to the pot with 1 cup of water. Boil it over high heat. Mash it as you can.
- After five minutes, the juice will be released. Remove the mixture from the heat.
- Pour the blackberry pulp through a cheesecloth-lined strainer.
- Add ¾ cup of cane sugar and stir well. Add this mixture into the jam pot and boil it.
- Pour this mixture into the jars. Leave ½-inch space.
- Seal it. Remove any air bubbles.
- Place the hot jelly jar into the water bath canner. Process for 10 minutes.

NUTRITION

Calories 34, Protein 1g,
Carbohydrate 9g, Fat 1g,
Sugar 8g

PEAR JELLY

Prep time: 5 min
Cook time: 5 min

Serving: 20

INGREDIENTS:

- 4 cups pear juice
- 2 tbsp lemon juice
- 2 cups sugar
- 3 tsp pectin
- 3 tsp calcium water

DIRECTIONS:

- Add calcium water, lemon juice, and pear juice into the pot and boil it.
- Add sugar and pectin and combine well.
- Add this mixture to the boiling juice and boil it for 2 to 3 minutes. Remove from the heat.
- Add this mixture to the jars. Process it into the water bath canner for 5 minutes.
- Store it in the fridge.

NUTRITION

Calories 63, Protein 0g, Carbohydrate 25g, Fat 0g, Sugar 25g

PEACH JELLY

Prep time: 5 min
Cook time: 10 min

Serving: 20

INGREDIENTS:

- 3 cups peach juice
- ½ cup lemon juice
- 1 packet pectin
- 5 cups sugar

DIRECTIONS:

- Add peaches into the pot and boil it for 20 to 30 minutes. Strain a jelly bag into the bowl.
- Boil the lemon juice and peach juice over high heat. Add sugar and powdered pectin and stir well. Again boil it for 1 minute.
- Add the mixture to the jars.
- Process it into the water bath canner for 10 minutes.
- Turn off the heat. Allow it to cool.
- Store it.

NUTRITION

Calories 47, Carbohydrate 12.2g, Fiber 0.1g, Sugar 12.1g

RED PEPPER JELLY

Prep time: 20 min
Cook time: 30 min

Serving: 20

INGREDIENTS:

- 3 cups red bell pepper, chopped
- 1 cup green bell pepper, chopped
- ¼ cup jalapeño pepper, chopped
- 1 cup apple cider vinegar
- 1 oz pectin powder
- 5 cups white sugar

DIRECTIONS:

- Add jalapeno, green, and red bell pepper into the saucepan and place it over high heat. Add pectin and apple cider vinegar and mix well. Add sugar and stir well. Again boil for 2 to 3 minutes. Remove from the heat.
- Add jelly into the jars and place the lid on.
- Place the jars into the water bath canner and process for 5 minutes.

NUTRITION

Calories 206, Protein 1g,
Carbohydrate 52g, Fat 1g,
Sugar 51g

LEMON JELLY

Prep time: 10 min
Cook time: 20 min

Serving: 4

INGREDIENTS:

- 2 cups squeezed lemon juice
- 1 cup squeezed clementine juice
- ¾ cup sugar

DIRECTIONS:

- Sterilize the jars.
- Squeeze the lemons to get juice and clementines to get juice. Strain the juice to remove the pulp.
- Add juice to the pot. Add sugar and boil it for 10 minutes.
- Add jelly to the frozen saucer and wait for 30 seconds.
- Pour the jelly into the sterilized jars and seal them.
- Process it into the water bath canner for 10 minutes.
- Store it.

NUTRITION

Calories 805, Protein 1g,
Carbohydrate 209g, Fat 1g,
Sugar 201g

APPLE JELLY

 Prep time: 10 min
Cook time: 20 min

 Serving: 4

INGREDIENTS:

- 3 cups unsweetened apple juice
- 4 tbsp pectin
- ½ tsp butter
- 3 1/3 cups granulated sugar

DIRECTIONS:

- Add apple juice into the saucepan and place it over medium heat. Add pectin and butter and stir well.
- Boil it over high heat. Add sugar and boil hard for 1 minute.
- Add hot jelly into the sterilized jars. Wipe the rims and seal them.
- Place the jars into the water bath canner.
- Process for 10 minutes.
- Store it.

NUTRITION

Calories 59, Protein 0g, Carbohydrate 15.3g, Fat 0g, Sugar 15.3g

WATERMELON JELLY

Prep time: 10 min
Cook time: 20 min

Serving: 4

INGREDIENTS:

- 4 cups watermelon juice, 4 cups
- 4 cups sugar, 4 cups
- 1 packet pectin
- ¼ cup lemon juice

NUTRITION

Calories 100, Protein 1g, Carbohydrate 22g, Fat 0g, Sugar 22g

DIRECTIONS:

- Add watermelon into the blender and strain the mixture.
- Add the juice to the pot and place it over medium-high heat.
- Add sugar and pectin and stir well. Add remaining sugar and stir well.
- Again boil for 1-2 minutes. Add lemon juice and stir well.
- Remove from the heat. Add it into the jars.
- Place the jars into the water bath canner and process for 5 minutes.
- Remove the jars from the canner.
- Store it.

JAM
RECIPES

PEAR JAM

Prep time: 20 min
Cook time: 15 min

Serving: 8 1/2 jars

INGREDIENTS:

- 1 tsp ground cinnamon
- ½ tsp ground nutmeg
- ½ tsp ground cloves
- 4 ½ cups mashed ripe pears
- 3 tbsp powdered fruit pectin
- ¼ cup lemon juice
- ½ tsp ground allspice
- 7 ½ cups white sugar
- 1 tsp butter

NUTRITION

Calories 99, Protein 0g,
Carbohydrate 25g, Fat 0g,
Sugar 25g

DIRECTIONS:

- Firstly, add lemon juice, pears, nutmeg, fruit pectin, allspice, cinnamon, and cloves into the pot and bring to a boil. Stir well.
- Add sugar and bring to a boil for one minute. Then, add butter and mix well.
- After that, for five minutes, sterilize the jars and lids in the boiled water.
- Place the pears jam into hot and sterilized jars and remove any air bubbles. Wipe the rims of the jars with a paper towel. Place lids tightly.
- Add water into the water bath canner and bring to a boil. Place jars in it and bring to a boil. Add more water if needed. Cover the canner and process for 10 minutes.
- Remove jars from the water bath canner and place them onto the wooden surface.
- Let's cool it. When cooled, press the top of each lid with your fingers.
- Make sure that the seal is tight.
- Let it cool in a calm and dark area like a kitchen cabinet.

JALAPENO STRAWBERRY JAM

Prep time: 40 min
Cook time: 20 min

Serving: 8 1/2 jars

INGREDIENTS:

- 7 cups white sugar
- 2 ounces powdered fruit pectin
- 1 cup jalapeno peppers, minced
- ¼ cup lemon juice
- 4 cups crushed strawberries

DIRECTIONS:

- Add pectin, lemon juice, crushed strawberries, and minced jalapeno pepper into the saucepan and boil on high heat.
- Add sugar and stir until sugar is dissolved. Bring to a boil and cook for one minute.
- After that, for five minutes, sterilize the jars and lids in the boiled water.
- Place jam into the hot and sterilized jars and wipe the rims with a paper towel. Place lids tightly.
- Add water to the stockpot and boil on high heat.
- Place jars into the water bath canner and bring to a boil. Cover the water bath canner and process it for ten minutes.
- Remove the jars from the water bath canner and place them onto the wooden surface. Let cool overnight. When cooled, press the top of each lid with your fingers. Make sure that the seal is tight.
- Let's store it in a cool and dark area.

NUTRITION

Calories 90, Protein 0g,
Carbohydrate 23g, Fat 0g,
Sugar 23g

BOURBON PEACH JAM

Prep time: 70 min
Cook time: 10 min

Serving: 3 1/2 jars

INGREDIENTS:

- 4 cups peaches, chopped and peeled
- 1 tbsp lemon juice
- 3 tbsp bourbon

DIRECTIONS:

- Add lemon juice and peaches into the saucepan and bring to a boil. Lower the heat and simmer for 60 minutes.
- Remove from the heat. Then, add bourbon and stir well.
- Place the hot mixture into the jars.
- Remove any air bubbles. Wipe rims. Apply bands.
- Prepare the water bath canner. Place lids on the jars. Add water into the water bath canner and bring to a boil. Place jars into the water bath canner and bring to a boil. Add more boiled water if required.
- Cover the water bath canner and process for 10 minutes. Remove the jars from the water bath canner. Let cool it. Make sure that the seal is tight.
- Remove jars from the canner.

NUTRITION

Calories 199, Protein 2g, Carbohydrate 51g, Fat 0g, Sugar 51g

BLUEBERRY JAM

Prep time: 15 min
Cook time: 20 min

Serving: 3 jars

INGREDIENTS:

- 21 oz blueberries
- 2 cups sugar
- 2 tbsp lemon juice

DIRECTIONS:

- Rinse and thoroughly dry blueberries.
- Add lemon juice, sugar, and blueberries to the saucepan and combine well. Turn the heat on low and stir for 5 to 8 minutes.
- Increase the heat to a rolling boil. Boil for 10 minutes.
- When done, turn off the heat. Allow it to stand for 30 seconds.
- Skim any scum off the top of the jam with a spoon.
- Allow the jam to sit for 5 minutes.
- Carefully ladle your jam into your hot jars and put the lids on immediately. Allow the jam to cool completely.
- Wipe the jars to remove spills, and store the jam in a cool, dark place.

NUTRITION

Calories 116, Protein 0g,
Carbohydrate 30g, Fat 0g,
Sugar 28g

APRICOT JAM

Prep time: 40 min
Cook time: 1 hr 20 min

Serving: 12 jars

INGREDIENTS:

- 5 lbs apricot
- ¼ cup water
- ¼ cup lemon juice
- 4lbs granulated sugar

DIRECTIONS:

- Wash the jars and lids. If washing by hand, use hot, soapy water and rinse them well.
- Rinse the apricot and pat dry, and remove any dirt. Then, cut them in half and remove the stones.
- Add apricot, water, and lemon juice into the saucepan and boil it.
- Cover the pot and cook for 10 to 15 minutes until tender.
- Add sugar and stir well until dissolved. Increase the heat and boil until the liquid is finished.
- When the jam looks thicker, turn off the heat.
- Allow it to stand for 10 minutes.
- Transfer it to the sterilized jars. Seal the jars tightly.
- Store the jam in a cool, dark place.
- Always use a clean, dry spoon to avoid contamination when using the jam. After opening a jar, as a further precaution, store it in the refrigerator.

NUTRITION

Calories 682, Protein 3g,
Carbohydrate 173g, Fat 1g,
Sugar 169g

RASPBERRY JAM

Prep time: 15 min
Cook time: 20 min

Serving: 3 jars

INGREDIENTS:

- 1/2 cup water
- 17 oz raspberries
- 2 cups sugar
- 2 tbsp lemon juice

DIRECTIONS:

- Rinse the raspberries in a colander and remove any dirt.
- Add water, lemon juice, sugar, and raspberries to the saucepan and combine well.
- Lower the heat and cook for 5 to 8 minutes.
- When sugar is dissolved, increase the heat to a rolling boil. Boil for 5 minutes.
- Turn off the heat. Allow it to stand for 30 seconds.
- Carefully ladle your jam into your hot jars and put the lids on immediately. Allow the jam to cool completely. Wipe the jars to remove spills, and store the jam in a cool, dark place.

NUTRITION

Calories 56, Protein 0g,
Carbohydrate 15g, Sugar
15g

PLUM JAM

Prep time: 30 min
Cook time: 40 min

Serving: 11 jars

INGREDIENTS:

- 4 ½ lbs plums, sliced
- ½ cup water
- 3 ½ lbs granulated sugar
- 1 ½ tbsp lemon juice

DIRECTIONS:

- Rinse the plums in a colander and remove any dirt.
- Add water, lemon juice, sugar, and plums to the saucepan and combine well.
- Lower the heat and cook for 15-20 minutes.
- When sugar is dissolved, increase the heat to a rolling boil. Boil for 5 to 15 minutes.
- Turn off the heat. Allow it to stand for 30 seconds.
- Carefully ladle your jam into your hot jars and put the lids on immediately. Allow the jam to cool completely. Wipe the jars to remove spills, and store the jam in a cool, dark place.

NUTRITION

Calories 612, Protein 1g,
Carbohydrate 157g, Fat 1g,
Sugar 154g

MANGO JAM

Prep time: 20 min
Cook time: 40 min

Serving: 11 jars

INGREDIENTS:

- 7 mangoes, with seed core, fresh
- 3 cups sugar
- 2 tbsp lemon juice

DIRECTIONS:

- Peel the mangoes and remove the peel.
- Add all sugar and lemon juice over mangoes and combine well.
- Add mangoes to the pot and cook for 30 minutes over low heat.
- Lower the heat and cook until the jam is thickened.
- Turn off the heat. Allow it to stand for 30 seconds.
- Ladle your jam into your hot and sterilized jars and put the lids on immediately.
- The jam will be good for ten months if unopened. Store in the fridge once opened.

NUTRITION

Calories 27, Protein 1g,
Carbohydrate 7g, Fat 1g,
Sugar 7g

ORANGE MARMALADE

Prep time: 20 min
Cook time: 40 min

Serving: 7

INGREDIENTS:

- 10-12 oranges, 10-12
- 2 lemons, 2
- 1 ½ quarts water
- 8 cups sugar

DIRECTIONS:

- Peel, thinly slice, and chop oranges, saving peels.
- Thinly slice the orange peels.
- Peel and thinly slice the lemon.
- Combine oranges, lemon, orange peel, and water in a pot and simmer for 5 minutes.
- Cover and let stand in a cool place for 12–18 hours.
- Start by preparing jars and getting water in the canner heating. When the jars are ready to be processed, you want the canner hot but not boiling.
- Boil the orange mixture until tender.
- Pour the marmalade into the sterilized and hot jar. Remove any air bubbles. Place the jar into the water bath canner. Process for 10-15 minutes.

NUTRITION

Calories 592, Protein 2g,
Carbohydrate 153g, Fat 1g,
Sugar 148g

SWEET CHERRY JAM

Prep time: 10 min
Cook time: 15 min

Serving: 6 1/2 jars

INGREDIENTS:

- 1 quart cherries, chopped
- 4 ½ cups sugar
- ¼ cup lemon juice
- 1 packet powdered pectin
- ¼ tsp butter

DIRECTIONS:

- Rinse, pit, and chop cherries.
- Add pectin, lemon juice, and cherries to the pot and boil it.
- Add sugar and butter and boil for 2 minutes.
- Remove from heat. Fill the jar with jam and remove any air bubbles.
- Place the jars into the water bath canner. Process for 15 minutes.
- Leave them alone for about 12 hours.

NUTRITION

Calories 599, Protein 2g,
Carbohydrate 154g, Fat 1g,
Sugar 147g

GRAPE JAM

Prep time: 10 min
Cook time: 15 min

Serving: 2 jars

INGREDIENTS:

- 1 1/3 cups grape pulp
- 1/3 cup fruit juice or water
- 1 ½ tbsp pectin
- , ½ cup sugar

DIRECTIONS:

- Rinse the grapes.
- Add pectin, lemon juice, and grapes to the pot and boil it.
- Add sugar, water, and pectin and boil for 2 minutes.
- Remove from heat. Fill the jar with jam and remove any air bubbles.
- Place the jars into the water bath canner. Process for 15 minutes.
- Leave them alone for about 12 hours.

NUTRITION

Calories 33, Protein 0g,
Carbohydrate 9g, Fat 0g,
Sugar 8g

PEACH JAM

Prep time: 10 min
Cook time: 15 min

Serving: 6 jars

INGREDIENTS:

- 6 cups peaches, chopped
- 5 cups sugar
- 2 tbsp lemon juice
- 1 stick cinnamon
- ¼ tsp whole or ground allspice
- 2-3 whole cloves

DIRECTIONS:

- Peel and chop the peaches.
- Add allspice, cloves, and cinnamon stick to the pot and boil it.
- Add sugar, water, and pectin and boil for 2 minutes.
- Discard cinnamon stick.
- Remove from heat. Fill the jar with jam and remove any air bubbles.
- Place the jars into the water bath canner. Process for 15 minutes.
- Leave them alone for about 12 hours.
- Store it in a cool and dark place.

NUTRITION

Calories 47, Protein 0g,
Carbohydrate 12.2g, Fat 0g,
Sugar 12.1g

GINGER MARMALADE

Prep time: 10 min
Cook time: 15 min

Serving: 5 1/2 jars

INGREDIENTS:

- 3 ounces liquid pectin
- 4 cups water
- 3 ½ cups fresh ginger, peeled
- 5 cups white sugar

DIRECTIONS:

- Cut ginger in half, place it into the food processor, and process until smooth.
- Add crushed ginger into the saucepan and boil on medium heat. Lower the heat and cover the pot. Let simmer for 1 hour and 15 minutes.
- Add more water if required. Place cooked ginger in the strainer into the bowl with the retained bowl.
- Let cool for 4 hours.
- When cooled, place it into the pot. Add sugar and stir well and place it on medium-high heat. Bring to a boil for one minute.
- Add liquid pectin and cook for 7 minutes more.
- After that, for five minutes, sterilize the jars and lids in the boiled water. Place marmalade into the hot and sterilized jars and wipe the rims with a paper towel. Place lids tightly.
- Add water into the water bath canner and boil on high heat. Place jars into the water bath canner. Bring to a boil. Add more water if needed. Cover the water bath canner and process it for 15 minutes.
- Remove jars from the water bath canner and place them onto the wooden surface. When cooled, press the top of each lid with your fingers. Make sure that the seal is tight. Let's store it in a cool and dark area.

NUTRITION

Calories 138, Protein 0g,
Carbohydrate 35g, Fat 0g,
Sugar 34g

STRAWBERRY MARMALADE

Prep time: 20 min
Cook time: 30 min

Serving: 10 jars

INGREDIENTS:

- ½ cup water
- 2 lemons
- 2 oranges
- 1 quart strawberries, crushed
- 1/8 tsp baking soda
- 7 cups sugar
- 6 ounces liquid pectin

NUTRITION

Calories 349, Protein 1g,
Carbohydrate 90g, Fat 0g,
Sugar 87g

DIRECTIONS:

- Firstly, peel the lemon and orange and keep them aside. Remove the white membrane from the fruit and remove it. Keep it aside. Let chop the peels and place them into the saucepan with water and baking soda. Cover the pan with a lid and bring it to a boil. Let simmer for 10 minutes.
- Meanwhile, section the lemons and oranges and reserve juice. Add juice and fruit into the saucepan and cover the pan with a lid. Let simmer for 20 minutes. Then, add strawberries and 4 cups of fruit to the pan. Add sugar and combine it well. Bring to a boil without a lid for 5 minutes. Add pectin and stir well. Let boil for 1 minute. Stir well.
- Remove it from the heat. Place marmalade into the hot and sterilized jars and remove any air bubbles. Wipe the rims of the jars and place their lids tightly.
- Add water into the water bath canner and bring to a boil. Place jars into the water bath canner and bring to a boil. Cover the water bath canner and process for 10 minutes.
- Remove the jars from the water bath canner and cool them.

ORANGE CRANBERRY MARMALADE

 Prep time: 20 min
Cook time: 5 min

 Serving: 10 jars

INGREDIENTS:

- 2 tbsp lemon juice
- Zest of 1 lemon
- 4 ½ cups sugar
- 4 oranges
- ¾ cup water
- 1 cup cranberries, chopped
- 1.75 ounces fruit pectin

NUTRITION

Calories 648, Protein 1g,
Carbohydrate 165g, Fat 1g,
Sugar 156g

DIRECTIONS:

- Firstly, remove the zest from the lemon and oranges with a zester. You can use a vegetable peeler to remove the zest from lemons and oranges. Cut the peel into silvers and transfer it to the bowl. Keep it aside.
- Cut off the remaining oranges and chop them. Reserve juice. Transfer the orange and juice to a medium bowl.
- Add 1 cup of chopped cranberries to the oranges and stir well.
- Transfer 2 1/3 cups of fruit mixture to the pot. Add sugar to the pot and stir well. Elevate the heat to medium-high and stir frequently.
- Bring to a boil for 30 seconds, and stir constantly. Remove from the heat.
- Add ¾ cup of water into the saucepan. Add pectin and stir well. Bring to a boil for 1 minute, and stir well.
- Add lemon juice, orange zest, lemon zest, and hot pectin to the fruit mixture and stir for 3 minutes.
- Transfer the marmalade into the jars and remove any air bubbles.
- Wipe the rims of the jars and place their lids tightly. Add water into the water bath canner and bring to a boil. Place jars into the water bath canner and bring to a boil. Cover the water bath canner and process for 10 minutes. Remove the jars from the water bath canner and cool them.

CARROT AND LEMON MARMALADE

Prep time: 10 min
Cook time: 40 min

Serving: 3 jars

INGREDIENTS:

- 1 tsp ground cardamom
- 1 tbsp ginger, grated
- ¾ cup sugar
- 2 cups water
- ½ lb lemons
- 1lb carrots, peeled

DIRECTIONS:

- Rinse lemon under running water and remove the hard blossom ends and blemishes on the skin. Cut in half lengthwise and place it onto the cutting board. Cut lemon halves thinly and remove seeds.
- Add carrots to the food processor and grate them.
- Add grated carrots, lemons, and water into the saucepan and cover the pan with a lid. Let sit at room temperature overnight.
- Add cardamom, ginger, and sugar into the carrot mixture and place the pan on medium heat. Bring to a boil. Lower the heat and simmer for 45 to 50 minutes until thickened.
- Remove the pan from the heat.
- Rinse the jars and place marmalade into the jars. Wipe the rims with a paper towel. Place lids and bands and cover them tightly.
- Wipe the rims of the jars and place their lids tightly.
- Add water into the water bath canner and bring to a boil. Place jars into the water bath canner and bring to a boil. Cover the water bath canner and process for 10 minutes.
- Remove the jars from the water bath canner and cool them.

NUTRITION

Calories 56, Protein 1g,
Carbohydrate 14g, Fat 1g,
Sugar 13g

RED PEPPER MARMALADE

Prep time: 10 min
Cook time: 30 min

Serving: 3 jars

INGREDIENTS:

- 1 tsp red chili flakes
- 500g sugar
- Water, as needed
- 1 red bell pepper
- 1 orange
- 1 lemon

DIRECTIONS:

- Rinse citrus fruits under clean water and pat them dry. Remove stalks from the pepper, cut them into chunks, and remove the membrane inside the peppers.
- Cut the orange into 8 chunks and slice the lemon into 4 pieces.
- Add them to the food processor and pulse until smooth.
- Place fruit into the jug and measure out the same amount in water. Then, add dried chili flakes, water, and fruit to the pan and place it on medium heat. Let simmer for 20-30 minutes.
- When tender, remove the heat and clean the pan with a clean towel. Let sit overnight.
- Add sugar into the pan, place it on medium heat, and stir until dissolved. Bring to a boil for 10 minutes.
- After that, sterilize the jars and lids in the water bath canner for five minutes.
- Place marmalade into the hot and sterilized jars and wipe the rims with a paper towel. Place lids tightly.
- Wipe the rims of the jars and place their lids tightly. Add water into the water bath canner and bring to a boil. Place jars into the water bath canner and bring to a boil. Cover the water bath canner and process for 10 minutes. Remove the jars from the water bath canner and cool them.

NUTRITION

Calories 26, Protein 0.2g,
Carbohydrate 5.9g, Fat 0.3g

FIG AND LEMON MARMALADE

Prep time: 10 min
Cook time: 1 hr 45 min

Serving: 3 jars

INGREDIENTS:

- 1 tsp black pepper
- 4 cups sugar
- 500g figs
- 3 lemons

DIRECTIONS:

- Firstly, cut off the stalks of the figs and cut them into quarters.
- Cut lemons in half, lengthwise.
- Place fruit into the bowl and cover with water. Place a clean tea towel over the bowl. Let sit overnight.
- Add fruit mix into the pan the next day and simmer for 1 ½ hours.
- Add black pepper and sugar and stir until dissolved. Bring to a boil for 10 minutes.
- After that, sterilize the jars and lids in the water bath canner for five minutes.
- Place marmalade into the hot and sterilized jars and wipe the rims of the jars with a paper towel. Place lids tightly. Wipe the rims of the jars and place their lids tightly.
- Add water into the water bath canner and bring to a boil. Place jars into the water bath canner and bring to a boil. Cover the water bath canner and process for 10 minutes.
- Remove the jars from the water bath canner and cool them.

NUTRITION

Calories 1446, Protein 3g, Carbohydrate 376g, Fat 1g, Sugar 362g

BEET MARMALADE

Prep time: 10 min
Cook time: 1 hr 30 min

Serving: 2 jars

INGREDIENTS:

- 4 red beets, roasted and peeled
- 1 ½ cups sugar
- 1 lemon
- 2 tbsp ginger, chopped

DIRECTIONS:

- Firstly, trim down the stalks and remove the thin root end.
- Wrap the beet with foil and put it onto the baking sheet. Place it into the oven and cook for 45 minutes to one minute. Let it cool, and then peel it.
- Add beet to the food processor and pulse until chopped.
- Transfer the beets to the saucepan. Then, add sugar and stir well.
- Cut the lemon into big chunks and add it into the food processor with chopped ginger. Blend until smooth.
- Place it into the saucepan and cook on medium-low heat.
- Place hot marmalade into the hot and sterilized jars.
- Add water into the water bath canner and bring to a boil. Place jars into the water bath canner and bring to a boil. Cover the water bath canner and process for 15 minutes.
- Remove the jars from the water bath canner and cool them.

NUTRITION

Calories 16, Protein 0g, Carbohydrate 2g, Fat 1g, Sugar 2g

PRESERVES
RECIPES

MULBERRY PRESERVES

Prep time: 10 min
Cook time: 20 min

Serving: 8 jars

INGREDIENTS:

- 2 cups of water, plus 1 tbsp
- 6 cups mulberries
- ¾ cup white sugar
- 1.75 oz powdered fruit pectin
- 3 oz strawberry flavor gelatin

NUTRITION

Calories 28, Protein 0g,
Carbohydrate 7g, Fat 0g,
Sugar 7g

DIRECTIONS:

- Firstly, add 1 tbsp of water and 6 cups mulberries into the big pot and bring to a boil. Then, lower the heat and cover the pot with a lid. Let simmer for 15 to 20 minutes. Mash the mulberries with a potato masher.
- Add sugar, 2 cups of water, powdered fruit pectin, and strawberry flavor gelatin into the medium bowl and stir until dissolved.
- Add gelatin mixture into the mashed mulberries and bring to a boil.
- After that, sterilize the jars and lids into the boiled water for five minutes. Place boiled mulberries mixture into the hot jars and remove any air bubbles from the jar.
- Wipe the jars with a paper towel or moist pepper towel and place lids and tightly packed as you can.
- Add water into the water bath canner and bring to a boil. Place jars into the water bath canner. Add more boiled water if required. Cover the water bath canner and process for 15 minutes.
- After 15 minutes, remove the jars from the water bath canner and put them onto the wood surface until cool.
- When cooked, press the top of each lid with your fingers and ensure that the seal is tight.
- You can store it in a cool and dark area like a kitchen cupboard.

PEACH PRESERVES

Prep time: 20 min
Cook time: 1 hr

Serving: 8 jars

INGREDIENTS:

- 12 fresh peaches, pitted and chopped
- 2 oz dry pectin
- 4 ½ cups white sugar

DIRECTIONS:

- Firstly, chop one cup of peaches and place them into the big saucepan. Then, add the remaining peaches and place them over medium-low heat. Bring to a boil and cook for 20 minutes.
- Place sugar and bring to a boil over medium heat.
- Add dry pectin and boil for one minute.
- Remove it from the heat.
- After that, sterilize the jars and lids into the boiled water for five minutes.
- Place mixture into the sterilized jars and process it into the boiling water bath canner for ten minutes.
- Let cool it and store it in a dark and cool place.

NUTRITION

Calories 78, Protein 0.2g,
Carbohydrate 20g, Fat 0.1g,
Sugar 20g

BLUEBERRY PRESERVES

Prep time: 5 min
Cook time: 25 min

Serving: 8 jars

INGREDIENTS:

- 2 ½ cups fresh blueberries
- 1 ¼ cups granulated sugar
- 1 tbsp lemon juice
- 1 tsp fresh lemon zest

DIRECTIONS:

- Add lemon zest, lemon juice, sugar, and blueberries to the saucepan and boil it. Press the blueberries with a potato masher. Boil for 15 to 20 minutes.
- Pour the preserved into the sterilized jar.
- Place mixture into the sterilized jars and process it into the boiling water bath canner for 15 minutes.
- Let cool it and store it in a dark and cool place.

NUTRITION

Calories 49, Carbohydrates 12g, Potassium 11mg, Sugar 11g

STRAWBERRY PRESERVES

Prep time: 5 min
Cook time: 25 min

Serving: 6

INGREDIENTS:

- 4 cups strawberries, hulled
- 2/3 cup granulated sugar
- 1 lemon, zest and juiced

DIRECTIONS:

- Cut the strawberries in half.
- Add strawberries, sugar, lemon juice, and lemon zest to the saucepan and boil it over medium heat.
- Place mixture into the sterilized jars and process it into the boiling water bath canner for 15 minutes.
- Wipe the rim, cover and seal, and then allow it to cool completely before storing in refrigerator until needed.

NUTRITION

Calories 122, Protein 1g,
Carbohydrate 31g, Fat 1g,
Sugar 27g

TOMATO PRESERVE

Prep time: 10 min
Cook time: 1 hr

Serving: 16

INGREDIENTS:

- 2 lbs ripe tomatoes
- ¾ cup brown sugar
- ¼ cup lemon juice
- 1 tbsp ginger, grated
- 1 ½ tsp salt
- ½ tsp ground cumin
- ½ tsp red pepper, crushed
- ½ tsp garlic powder

DIRECTIONS:

- Chop the tomatoes and remove any seeds. Grate the ginger.
- Add all ingredients to the saucepan and simmer for 15 minutes.
- Allow it to sit for 12 hours.
- Place mixture into the sterilized jars and process it into the boiling water bath canner for 20 minutes.
- Wipe the rim, cover and seal, and then allow it to cool completely before storing in refrigerator until needed.

NUTRITION

Calories 51, Protein 1g,
Carbohydrate 13g, Fat 1g,
Sugar 12g

PRESERVED FIGS

Prep time: 10 min
Cook time: 20 min

Serving: 8

INGREDIENTS:

- 1lb figs
- ¾ cup sugar
- 3 tbsp lemon juice
- ¼ cup bourbon
- 1 vanilla bean
- 1 star anise
- 4 cloves
- 4 peppercorn
- 1 tsp allspice

DIRECTIONS:

- Rinse the figs under cold water.
- Add figs to the stockpot with spices, bourbon, lemon juice, and sugars and simmer over low heat for 10 minutes.
- Place mixture into the sterilized jars and process it into the boiling water bath canner for 10 minutes.
- Cool 12 hours. Test seals. Label and store jars.

NUTRITION

Calories 137, Protein 1g,
Carbohydrate 31g, Fat 1g,
Sugar 28g

CHERRY PRESERVES

Prep time: 5 min
Cook time: 15 min

Serving: 4

INGREDIENTS:

- 1lb cherries, pitted
- 1 ½ cups granulated sugar
- 1 tbsp lemon juice, freshly squeezed
- ½ tsp lemon zest
- 1 tbsp butter

DIRECTIONS:

- Rinse and prepare the cherries.
- Add lemon juice, lemon zest, granulated sugar, and cherries to the saucepan and boil it for 5 minutes.
- Increase the heat and boil for 3 minutes. Then, remove from the heat. Add butter and stir well.
- Transfer the mixture into the sterilized jars and process it into the boiling water bath canner for 10-15 minutes.
- Leave to cool slightly and carefully transfer the jam into a clean, tempered jar.
- Once cooled, cover and refrigerate.

NUTRITION

Calories 129, Protein 0.4g,
Carbohydrate 31g, Fat 1g,
Sugar 30g

PEAR PRESERVES

Prep time: 5 min
Cook time: 2 hrs

Serving: 7

INGREDIENTS:

- 16 cups pears
- 4 cups sugar
- 2 cups water
- 3 tbsp lemon juice

DIRECTIONS:

- Add lemon juice, water, sugar, and pears to the stockpot and boil it for 1 ½ to 2 hours. Then, remove from heat.
- Pour the mixture into the hot and sterilized jars, leaving ¼-inch space and remove any air bubbles. Wipe around the jars to clean, center the lids. Seal it tightly.
- Place the jars into the water bath canner and process for 10 minutes.
- Store it in a dark and cool place.

NUTRITION

Calories 79, Protein 0g,
Carbohydrate 21g, Fat 0g,
Sugar 25g

APRICOT RASPBERRY PRESERVES

Prep time: 5 min
Cook time: 27 min

Serving: 2

INGREDIENTS:

- 1lb apricots
- 1 tsp lemon juice
- 1/3 cup granulated sugar
- 1/2 cup raspberries

DIRECTIONS:

- Add apricot, lemon juice, and sugar to the food processor and pulse until smooth.
- Transfer the mixture to the pan and boil for 1-2 minutes.
- Pour the mixture into the hot and sterilized jars, leaving ¼-inch space and remove any air bubbles. Wipe around the jars to clean, center the lids. Seal it tightly.
- Place the jars into the water bath canner and process for 10 minutes.
- Store it in a dark and cool place.

NUTRITION

Calories 498, Protein 6.6g, Carbohydrate 123g, Fat 0.2g, Sugar 23g

ORANGE PRESERVES

Prep time: 20 min
Cook time: 40 min

Serving: 7

INGREDIENTS:

- 10-12 oranges
- 2 lemons, 2
- 1 ½ quarts water
- 8 cups sugar

DIRECTIONS:

- Peel, thinly slice, and chop oranges, saving peels.
- Thinly slice the orange peels.
- Peel and thinly slice the lemon.
- Combine oranges, lemon, orange peel, and water in a pot and simmer for 5 minutes.
- Cover and let stand in a cool place for 12–18 hours.
- Start by preparing jars and getting water in the canner heating. When the jars are ready to be processed, you want the canner hot but not boiling.
- Boil the orange mixture until tender.
- Pour the marmalade into the sterilized and hot jar. Remove any air bubbles. Place the jar into the water bath canner. Process for 10-15 minutes.

NUTRITION

Calories 592, Protein 2g,
Carbohydrate 153g, Fat 1g,
Sugar 148g

SAUCES & SALSA RECIPES

PEACH SALSA

Prep time: 25 min
Cook time: 15 min

Serving: 8 jars

INGREDIENTS:

- ¼ cup lime juice
- ½ cup cold water
- 1 cup red bell pepper, chopped
- 6 cups peaches, peeled
- 1 cup granulated sugar
- ½ cup red onion, chopped
- 1 cup apple cider vinegar
- 2 garlic cloves, minced
- 2 jalapeno peppers, seeded and chopped
- ½ tsp kosher salt
- Habanero pepper, 1, seeded and minced
- ¼ cup coriander, chopped

DIRECTIONS:

- Firstly, toss all ingredients except coriander.
- Place all ingredients into the Dutch oven and bring to a boil on high heat. Lower the heat and cook for 5 minutes. Remove from the heat. Then, add coriander and stir well.
- Place peach jam into the sterilized jars and remove any air bubbles.
- Wipe the rims of each jar and place lids tightly.
- Add water into the water bath canner and bring to a boil. Place jars into the water bath canner and process them for 15 minutes.
- Remove the lid from the water bath canner. Let the jars stand for 5 minutes.
- Store it in the fridge.

NUTRITION

Calories 46, Protein 1g, Carbohydrate 12g, Fat 1g, Sugar 9g

PLUM HABANERO SALSA

Prep time: 10 min
Cook time: 50 min

Serving: 4 jars

INGREDIENTS:

- 2 lbs tomatoes, cored and halved
- 2 garlic cloves, minced
- 1 red onion, diced
- 3lbs plums, pitted and diced
- 2 tbsp tequila
- 1/3 cup lime juice
- 1 tsp salt
- 2 tsp coriander seeds, toasted and crushed
- 2-3 Habaneros, minced

NUTRITION

Calories 32, Protein 1g,
Carbohydrate 7g, Fat 1g,
Sugar 6g

DIRECTIONS:

- Preheat the oven to 350 degrees Fahrenheit.
- Halve tomatoes and place them onto the baking sheet. Put it to the oven and roast for 20 minutes. Flip tomatoes and roast for 10 minutes more. Let cool it. Then, chop it. Mix tomatoes with the remaining ingredient, add them into the pot, and bring to a boil for 20 minutes. Place hot salsa into the jars. Remove any air bubbles. Wipe rims. Apply bands.
- Prepare the water bath canning. Add water into the water bath canner and bring to a boil. Place jars into the water bath canner and process it for 20 minutes.
- Remove the jars from the water bath canner. Let the jars stand for 5 minutes.

CORN AND CHERRY TOMATO SALSA

 Prep time: 10 min
Cook time: 50 min

 Serving: 6 jars

INGREDIENTS:

- 5 lbs. cherry tomatoes, chopped
- 2 cups corn kernels
- 1 cup red onion, chopped
- 2 tsp salt
- ½ cup bottled lime juice
- 2 jalapeno peppers, seeded and minced
- 1 tsp chipotle chili powder
- ½ cup cilantro, chopped

DIRECTIONS:

- Add all ingredients into the saucepan and bring to a boil for 5 to 10 minutes.
- Place hot salsa into the hot and sterilized jars. Remove any air bubbles. Wipe the rims and place lids on the jar. Apply the band.
- Prepare the water bath canning. Add water into the water bath canner and bring to a boil. Place jars into the water bath canner and process them for 15 minutes.
- Remove the jars from the water bath canner. Let cool jars for 5 minutes.

NUTRITION

Calories 48, Protein 1.1g, Carbohydrate 10.2g, Fat 0.8g, Sugar 4.7g

SPAGHETTI MARINARA SAUCE

Prep time: 2 hrs
Cook time: 2 hrs

Serving: 4 jars

INGREDIENTS:

- ½ cup vegetable or canola oil
- 18 oz tomato paste
- 12 cups tomatoes, peeled, drained, and chopped
- 2 cups white or yellow onions, chopped
- 1 cup green bell pepper, chopped
- 1 cup red bell pepper, chopped
- ¼ to ½ cup granulated or brown sugar
- 3 tbsp salt
- 2 tbsp minced garlic
- 1 ½ tbsp dried oregano
- 1 ½ tbsp dried basil
- 1 ½ tsp dried parsley
- 2 tsp Worcestershire sauce
- 1 bay leaf
- ½ cup lemon juice

NUTRITION

Calories 180, Protein 5g,
Carbohydrate 22g, Fat 10g,
Sugar 12g

DIRECTIONS:

- Firstly, mix all ingredients except lemon juice into the pot. Bring to a boil. Lower the heat and simmer for 1 hour. Discard bay leaf.
- Transfer the sauce to the blender and blend until smooth.
- Add 2 tbsp lemon juice into the hot and sterilized jars. Add spaghetti sauce over it. Wipe the rim of each jar with a clean and moist towel. Place a lid over it tightly.
- Add water into the water bath canner and bring to a boil. Place jars into the water bath canner and bring to a boil. Add more boiled water if required.
- Cover the water bath canner and process for 40 minutes.
- Remove the jars from the water bath canner. Let cool it. Make sure that the seal is tight.

GARLIC MUSTARD SAUCE

Prep time: 10 min
Cook time: 30 min

Serving: 8 jars

INGREDIENTS:

- 2lbs garlic
- 1/3 cup extra-virgin olive
- 1lb smith apples
- 2 cups apple juice
- 1lb Anaheim peppers
- 3 Serrano peppers
- ¼ cup mustard powder
- 2 tsp yellow mustard seeds
- 1 tsp coriander seeds
- 1 ½ cups white wine vinegar

NUTRITION

Calories 169, Protein 1g,
Carbohydrate 10g, Fat 14g,
Sugar 9g

DIRECTIONS:

- Peel and core apples. Let chop apples into pieces. Then, cut the tops off the garlic and cut them into pieces.
- Add apples and 1 cup of apple juice into the Dutch oven and simmer for 5 minutes; keep it aside.
- Place garlic bulbs onto the baking dish. Pour olive oil onto the garlic. Place it into the oven and bake it.
- Roast peppers under the broiler. Place roasted peppers into the zip-lock bag and close the lid. Let cool for 15 minutes. Remove stems and skins from the peppers.
- Add peppers, garlic, and apple mixture into the food processor and blend until smooth.
- Add one cup of apple juice, puree, and remaining ingredients into the saucepan and boil for 10 minutes.
- Place mixture into hot and sterilized jars. Remove air bubbles. Wipe rims. Apply bands.
- Add water into the water bath canner and bring to a boil. Place jars into the water bath canner and bring to a boil. Add more boiled water if required.
- Cover the water bath canner and process for 10 minutes. Remove the jars from the water bath canner. Let cool it. Make sure that the seal is tight.

TOMATO SAUCE

Prep time: 1 hr
Cook time: 1 hr

Serving: 14 cups

INGREDIENTS:

- 20 lbs tomatoes
- 7 tbsp lemon juice
- 1 tsp salt
- 3 ½ tsp dried basil

DIRECTIONS:

- Pick fresh tomatoes, cut them in half and remove the seeds.
- Add tomatoes to a cookie sheet and roast for 5 minutes at 350 degrees Fahrenheit.
- Remove skins and set them in a medium bowl.
- Add tomatoes to the food processor and pulse until smooth.
- Add tomato sauce to the pot and simmer until thickened.
- Transfer the sauce to the jars. Then, put it in a water bath canner. Process it for 35 minutes.
- Turn off the heat. Allow it to sit for 5 minutes in the water bath canner.
- Allow jars to rest untouched for at least 12 hours, 24 hours if you have the counter space.
- If any jars don't seal, store them in the refrigerator and use them within a day or two.)

NUTRITION

Calories 119, Protein 6g,
Carbohydrate 26g, Fat 1g,
Sugar 17g

PIZZA SAUCE

Prep time: 2 hrs
Cook time: 4 hrs

Serving: 24

INGREDIENTS:

- 15 lbs tomatoes
- 1 white onions, peeled and quartered
- 2 garlic cloves, chopped
- 1 tbsp olive oil
- 2 tsp salt
- 1 tbsp sugar
- 4 tbsp Italian seasoning
- 3 tsp lemon juice

DIRECTIONS:

- Transfer the onion and garlic to the food processor and pulse until smooth. Transfer the pureed onion and garlic to the pot. Add onion and cook for 5 minutes.
- Meanwhile, transfer the tomatoes to the food processor and pulse until pureed. Transfer it to the pot with Italian seasoning, sugar, and salt and cook for 4 hours.
- Add lemon juice to each jar. Add sauce to the Mason jars.
- Transfer the jars to the water bath canner with boiling water. Process for 20 minutes.
- Store it in a dark and cool place.

NUTRITION

Calories 63, Protein 3g,
Carbohydrate 13g, Fat 1g,
Sugar 8g

ROASTED CHIPOTLE SALSA

Prep time: 35 min
Cook time: 50 min

Serving: 6 jars

INGREDIENTS:

- 3 onions, cut in half and then quartered
- 3 green chilies, halved and seeded
- 4 jalapeno chilies, halved and seeded
- 9 garlic cloves, peeled
- 2 tbsp olive oil
- 6 lbs tomatoes, cored and cut in half
- 3 tbsp chipotle peppers in adobo
- 1 cup vinegar
- ¼ cup lime juice
- 2 tsp sea salt
- 2 tsp oregano
- 1 ½ tsp black pepper
- 1 ½ tsp ground cumin

DIRECTIONS:

- Preheat the oven to 450 degrees Fahrenheit.
- Place the garlic, onions, and peppers on a baking sheet and toss with 1 tbsp of olive oil.
- Drizzle the remaining 1 tbsp of oil on a baking sheet. Place the tomatoes and roast for 25 to 30 minutes.
- Remove the pans and cover them with foil for 10 minutes.
- Remove the tomato skin and chop it. Add tomatoes to the stock pot.
- Remove the foil from the pepper mixture. Remove the skin of the peppers with a sharp knife. Add all vegetables and chipotle peppers to the food processor and transfer them to the pot. Add remaining ingredients and boil for 20 minutes.
- Transfer the jars to the water bath canner with boiling water. Process for 20 minutes.
- Let cool for 12 or more hours before removing rings, testing lids for seal, labeling and storing in a cool, dark place for up to 18 months.

NUTRITION

Calories 33, Protein 1g, Carbohydrate 4g, Fat 1g, Sugar 2g

SPICY PLUM SAUCE

Prep time: 30 min
Cook time: 3 hrs

Serving: 6 jars

INGREDIENTS:

- 4 lbs plums, washed, cut in half and pitted
- ¾ cup onion, chopped
- 1 ½ cups brown sugar
- 1 cup white sugar
- 1 tbsp dry mustard
- 2 tbsp dry ground ginger
- 1 tbsp salt
- 2 garlic cloves, minced
- 2 tsp red pepper flakes
- 1 tsp ground cinnamon
- 1 cup cider vinega

DIRECTIONS:

- Chop the plums in the food processor and transfer them to the pot. Chop onions in the processor and transfer them to the pot. Add remaining ingredients with onions and plums and boil for 1 hour.
- Pour the sauce into hot jars, leaving 1/4-inch headspace. Attach lids and rings. Process for 20 minutes in a boiling-water canner. Turn off the heat, remove the lid and let jars sit in a canner to cool for 5 minutes. Remove to a cloth to cool completely.
- Test lids, label jars, store and use within a year to 18 months.

NUTRITION

Calories 24, Protein 1g,
Carbohydrate 6g, Fat 1g,
Sugar 6g

GREEN TOMATO SALSA

Prep time: 30 min
Cook time: 1 hr

Serving: 3-4 jars

INGREDIENTS:

- 2lbs green tomatoes, washed, husks removed
- 3 cups hot pepper
- 3 cups onions, chopped
- 6 garlic cloves, chopped
- 1 cup lime juice
- 2 tbsp dried oregano
- 1 tbsp salt
- 1 tbsp ground cumin
- 2 tsp black pepper

DIRECTIONS:

- Preheat the oven to 425 degrees Fahrenheit.
- Place the green tomatoes in the roasting pan. Roast for 30-35 minutes.
- Transfer it to the stockpot with the remaining ingredients. Simmer for 10 minutes.
- Pour the sauce into hot jars, leaving 1/4-inch headspace. Attach lids and rings. Process for 5 minutes in a boiling-water canner.
- Turn off the heat, remove the lid and let the jars sit in the canner to cool for 5 minutes. Remove to a cloth to cool completely.

NUTRITION

Calories 22, Protein 0.7g, Carbohydrate 4.7g, Fat 0.4g, Sugar 1.4g

SMOKEY CHERRY BBQ SAUCE

Prep time: 1 hr
Cook time: 45 min

Serving: 5 jars

INGREDIENTS:

- 3lbs sweet cherries
- 1 cup onion, chopped
- 3 garlic cloves, minced
- 1 cup apple cider vinegar
- ¾ cup honey
- 3 tsp salt
- 2 tsp Worcestershire sauce
- 2 tsp liquid smoke
- 2 tsp chili powder
- 1-2 tsp cayenne powder

DIRECTIONS:

- Rinse and pit cherries. Transfer them to the pot. Add garlic and onion and add them to the pot. Add remaining ingredients and stir well.
- Boil for 15 minutes over medium-low heat. Remove the lid and cook for 20 to 25 minutes until thickened.
- Transfer the mixture to the food processor and pulse until smooth.
- Return to low heat and cook for 10 to 15 minutes.
- Pour the sauce into hot jars, leaving 1/4-inch headspace. Attach lids and rings. Process for 5 minutes in a boiling-water canner.
- Remove the jars to a towel-lined surface to cool without moving for 24 hours.
- Store in a cool, dark place for 1 to 1 1/2 years

NUTRITION

Calories 62, Protein 0.2g, Carbohydrate 15.3g, Fiber 0.3g, Sugar 5.4g

CAPONATA SAUCE

Prep time: 1 hr 15 min
Cook time: 35 min

Serving: 6 jars

INGREDIENTS:

- 2lbs eggplants, stemmed and quartered lengthwise
- 4 lbs plum tomatoes, halved
- 2 red peppers, halved and seeded
- 2 onions, diced
- 2 celery ribs, diced
- 6 garlic cloves, minced
- ¼ cup water
- 1 ½ cups green olives, pitted and chopped
- ½ cup capers, drained
- 2 tbsp sugar
- 1 tbsp salt
- 2 tsp ground black pepper
- ½ cup red wine vinegar

DIRECTIONS:

- Preheat the oven to 375 degrees Fahrenheit.
- Arrange eggplant quarters and red pepper halves on a baking sheet.
- Spray the vegetable with oil. Place tomato halves on a rimmed baking sheet lined with foil. Roast for 25 to 30 minutes.
- Chop the tomatoes, red peppers, and eggplants.
- Add oil to the pot and heat it. Add tomatoes, celery, garlic, onions, and the remaining ingredients except for peppers and eggplant. Simmer for 20 minutes. Then, add peppers and eggplant and simmer for 5 minutes.
- Pour the sauce into hot jars, leaving 1/4-inch headspace. Attach lids and rings. Process for 35 minutes in a boiling-water canner.
- Remove jars and cool for 12-24 hours. Check lids for seal; they should not flex when the center is pressed.

NUTRITION

Calories 62, Protein 0.2g, Carbohydrate 15.3g, Fiber 0.3g, Sugar 5.4g

CHILI SAUCE

Prep time: 30 min
Cook time: 2 hrs

Serving: 6 jars

INGREDIENTS:

- 9 lbs tomatoes, peeled and chopped
- 6 onions, chopped
- 3 red bell peppers, seeded and chopped
- 6 red chilies, seeded and chopped
- 6 garlic cloves
- 2 cups apple cider vinegar
- 1 cup brown sugar
- 1 tbsp salt
- 1 tbsp mustard seed
- 1 tbsp horseradish, grated
- 2 tbsp chili powder
- 2 tsp allspice

NUTRITION

Calories 28, Protein 0g,
Carbohydrate 7g, Fat 0g,
Sugar 6g

DIRECTIONS:

- Place tomatoes, onions, red peppers, chilies and garlic in the food processor and pulse until smooth.
- Mix all ingredients in the pot and boil for 1 ½ to 2 hours.
- Pour the sauce into hot jars, leaving 1/4-inch headspace. Attach lids and rings. Process for 20 minutes in a boiling-water canner.
- Store in a cool, dark place.

CRANBERRY SAUCE

Prep time: 10 min
Cook time: 25 min

Serving: 2 jars

INGREDIENTS:

- 4 cups granulated sugar
- 4 cups water
- 8 cups fresh cranberries
- 1 orange

DIRECTIONS:

- Add water and sugar to the saucepan and boil for 5 minutes.
- Add cranberries and boil it. Lower the heat and boil for 15 minutes.
- Add orange zest and boil for a few minutes.
- Pour the cranberry sauce into hot jars.
- Remove air bubbles and wipe the rim.
- Place the jar in a boiling water canner. Process for 15 minutes.
- Turn off the heat, remove the lid, and let the jars stand for 5 minutes. Remove jars and cool for 12-24 hours. Check lids for seal; they should not flex when the center is pressed.

NUTRITION

Calories 103, Protein 0g,
Carbohydrate 27g, Fat 0g,
Sugar 24g

RASPBERRY SAUCE

Prep time: 10 min
Cook time: 5 min

Serving: 2 jars

INGREDIENTS:

- ½ cup unsweetened cocoa powder
- 6 tbsp pectin
- 4 ½ cups crushed red raspberries
- 6 ¾ cups granulated sugar
- 4 tbsp lemon juice

DIRECTIONS:

- Add lemon juice and raspberries to the saucepan and combine well.
- Add the pectin mixture and boil over high heat. Add sugar and boil for 1 minute. Remove from heat.
- Place the jar in a boiling water canner. Process for 10 minutes.
- Turn off the heat, remove the lid, and let the jars stand for 5 minutes. Remove jars and cool for 12-24 hours. Check lids for seal; they should not flex when the center is pressed.

NUTRITION

Calories 44, Protein 1g,
Carbohydrate 11g, Fat 0g,
Sugar 7g

DIJON MUSTARD

Prep time: 20 min
Cook time: 10 min

Serving: 6 jars

INGREDIENTS:

- 2 cups onion, chopped
- 2 cups dry white wine
- 1 cup white wine vinegar
- 1 tsp salt
- 6 garlic cloves, chopped
- 4 black peppercorns
- 1 sprig rosemary
- 1 cup yellow mustard seeds
- 1/3 cup dry mustard
- 2 2/3 cup water

DIRECTIONS:

- Add onion, dry white wine, white wine vinegar, salt, garlic, black peppercorn, and rosemary to the saucepan and boil for 15 to 20 minutes.
- Remove pan from heat. Pour the onion mixture through a strainer into a bowl. Discard solids. Add dry mustard and mustard seeds to the wine mixture. Allow it to sit for 24 hours.
- Add mustard mixture to the food processor and pulse until smooth.
- Transfer it to the saucepan and simmer for 5 minutes.
- Pour the sauce into the sterilized jars.
- Place the jar in a boiling water canner. Process for 10 minutes.
- Turn off the heat, remove the lid, and let the jars stand for 5 minutes.
- Remove jars and let cool.

NUTRITION

Calories 243, Protein 2.3g, Carbohydrate 5.5g, Fat 21g, Sugar 3.4g

HARISSA SAUCE

Prep time: 10 min
Cook time: 10 min

Serving: 3-4 jars

INGREDIENTS:

- 4 red peppers, roasted, peeled then diced
- 8 red chili, roasted, seeded then diced
- 1 onion, diced
- 6 garlic cloves, minced
- 1/3 cup tomato paste
- ¾ cup apple cider vinegar
- 1 tsp smoked paprika
- 1 tsp cumin seeds
- 1 tsp. sugar
- 2 tsp salt

DIRECTIONS:

- Add all ingredients to the saucepan and simmer for 10 minutes.
- Transfer it to the blender and blend until smooth.
- Pour the sauce into the sterilized jars.
- Place the jar in a boiling water canner. Process for 15 minutes.
- Turn off the heat, remove the lid, and let the jars stand for 5 minutes.
- Remove jars and cool for 12-24 hours. Check lids for seal; they should not flex when the center is pressed.

NUTRITION

Calories 13, Protein 0.1g, Carbohydrate 0.6g, Fat 1.3g, Sugar 0.2g

SWEET PINEAPPLE CHILI SAUCE

 Prep time: 10 min
Cook time: 10 min

 Serving: 3-4 jars

INGREDIENTS:

- 1 ½ cups pineapple
- ¾ cup pineapple juice
- 4 red chilies, stemmed and minced
- 4 garlic cloves, minced
- ½ cup vinegar
- 1 lime, zest and juiced
- 1 ½ cups sugar
- 1 tsp salt
- 1 tsp chili flakes

DIRECTIONS:

- Add all ingredients to the saucepan and simmer for 10 minutes until thickened.
- Ladle the sauce to the jars and remove any air bubbles. Place the jar in the water bath canner. Process for 15 minutes.
- Turn off the heat, remove the lid, and let the jars stand for 5 minutes. Remove jars and cool for 12-24 hours. Check lids for seal; they should not flex when the center is pressed.

NUTRITION

Calories 355, Carbohydrates 89g, Sodium 656mg, Sugar 81g

THAI SWEET CHILI DIPPING SAUCE

Prep time: 10 min
Cook time: 20 min

Serving: 3-4 jars

INGREDIENTS:

- ¼ cup garlic, chopped
- ½ tbsp salt
- 3 cups cider vinegar
- 3 cups sugar
- ¼ cup dried red chili flakes

DIRECTIONS:

- Add salt and garlic to the bowl and keep it aside.
- Add vinegar to the saucepan and boil it. Then, add sugar and stir well. Remove the vinegar and sugar mixture from the heat. Add garlic mixture and dried red chilies flakes and stir well.
- Ladle the sauce to the jars and remove any air bubbles. Place the jar in the water bath canner. Process for 20 minutes.
- Label the jars and store to a dark, cool cabinet for up to one year.

NUTRITION

Calories 32, Protein 1g,
Carbohydrate 8g, Fat 1g,
Sugar 8g

MANGO SAUCE

Prep time: 10 min
Cook time: 5 min

Serving: 3-4 jars

INGREDIENTS:

- 6 cups mangoes, diced
- 1 red onion, diced
- 1 ½ cups red bell pepper, seeded and diced
- 2 tsp fresh cilantro, chopped
- ½ tsp red pepper flakes, crushed
- 2 garlic cloves, minced
- 2 tsp ginger, chopped
- 1 cup brown sugar
- 1 ¼ cups vinegar
- ½ cup water

NUTRITION

Calories 151, Protein 1.5g,
Carbohydrate 36g, Fat 0.5g,
Sugar 32g

DIRECTIONS:

- Add all ingredients to the pot and boil for 5 minutes.
- Reduce the heat and simmer for 5 minutes.
- Ladle the sauce to the jars and remove any air bubbles. Place the jar in the water bath canner. Process for 15 minutes.
- Label the jars and store to a dark, cool cabinet for up to one year.

CHUTNEYS
RECIPES

PLUM CHUTNEY

Prep time: 30 min
Cook time: 3 hrs

Serving: 8 jars

INGREDIENTS:

- 4 lbs plums, washed, cut in half and pitted
- ¾ cup onion, chopped
- 1 ½ cups brown sugar
- 1 cup white sugar
- 1 tbsp dry mustard
- 2 tbsp dry ground ginger
- 1 tbsp salt
- 2 garlic cloves, minced
- 2 tsp red pepper flakes
- 1 tsp ground cinnamon
- 1 cup cider vinegar

DIRECTIONS:

- Chop the plums in the food processor and transfer them to the pot. Chop onions in the processor and transfer them to the pot. Add remaining ingredients with onions and plums and boil for 1 hour.
- Pour the sauce into hot jars, leaving 1/4-inch headspace. Attach lids and rings. Process for 20 minutes in a boiling-water canner. Turn off the heat, remove the lid and let jars sit in a canner to cool for 5 minutes. Remove to a cloth to cool completely.
- Test lids, label jars, store and use within a year to 18 months.

NUTRITION

Calories 24, Protein 1g, Carbohydrate 6g, Fat 1g, Sugar 6g

GREEN TOMATO CHUTNEY

Prep time: 30 min
Cook time: 3 hrs

Serving: 3-4 jars

INGREDIENTS:

- 2lbs green tomatoes, washed, husks removed
- 3 cups hot pepper
- 3 cups onions, chopped
- 6 garlic cloves, chopped
- 1 cup lime juice
- 2 tbsp dried oregano
- 1 tbsp salt
- 1 tbsp ground cumin
- 2 tsp black pepper

DIRECTIONS:

- Preheat the oven to 425 degrees Fahrenheit.
- Place the green tomatoes in the roasting pan. Roast for 30-35 minutes.
- Transfer it to the stockpot with the remaining ingredients. Simmer for 10 minutes.
- Pour the sauce into hot jars, leaving 1/4-inch headspace. Attach lids and rings. Process for 5 minutes in a boiling-water canner.
- Turn off the heat, remove the lid and let the jars sit in the canner to cool for 5 minutes. Remove to a cloth to cool completely.

NUTRITION

Calories 22, Protein 0.7g, Carbohydrate 4.7g, Fat 0.4g, Sugar 1.4g

MANGO CHUTNEY

Prep time: 10 min
Cook time: 5 min

Serving: 4 jars

INGREDIENTS:

- 6 cups mangoes, diced
- 1 red onion, diced
- 1 ½ cups red bell pepper, seeded and diced
- 2 tsp fresh cilantro, chopped
- ½ tsp red pepper flakes, crushed
- 2 garlic cloves, minced
- 2 tsp ginger, chopped
- 1 cup brown sugar
- 1 ¼ cups vinegar
- ½ cup water

DIRECTIONS:

- Add all ingredients to the pot and boil for 5 minutes.
- Reduce the heat and simmer for 5 minutes.
- Ladle the sauce to the jars and remove any air bubbles. Place the jar in the water bath canner. Process for 15 minutes.
- Label the jars and store to a dark, cool cabinet for up to one year.

NUTRITION

Calories 151, Protein 1.5g, Carbohydrate 36g, Fat 0.5g, Sugar 32g

PEACH CHUTNEY

Prep time: 25 min
Cook time: 15 min

Serving: 8 jars

INGREDIENTS:

- ¼ cup lime juice
- ½ cup cold water
- 1 cup red bell pepper, chopped
- 6 cups peaches, peeled
- 1 cup granulated sugar
- ½ cup red onion, chopped
- 1 cup apple cider vinegar
- 2 garlic cloves, minced
- 2 jalapeno peppers, seeded and chopped
- ½ tsp kosher salt
- Habanero pepper, 1, seeded and minced
- ¼ cup coriander, chopped

DIRECTIONS:

- Firstly, toss all ingredients except coriander.
- Place all ingredients into the Dutch oven and bring to a boil on high heat. Lower the heat and cook for 5 minutes. Remove from the heat. Then, add coriander and stir well.
- Place peach jam into the sterilized jars and remove any air bubbles.
- Wipe the rims of each jar and place lids tightly.
- Add water into the water bath canner and bring to a boil. Place jars into the water bath canner and process them for 15 minutes.
- Remove the lid from the water bath canner. Let the jars stand for 5 minutes.
- Store it in the fridge.

NUTRITION

Calories 46, Protein 1g,
Carbohydrate 12g, Fat 1g,
Sugar 9g

CRANBERRY CHUTNEY

Prep time: 10 min
Cook time: 25 min

Serving: 8 jars

INGREDIENTS:

- 4 cups granulated sugar
- 4 cups water
- 8 cups fresh cranberries
- 1 orange

DIRECTIONS:

- Add water and sugar to the saucepan and boil for 5 minutes.
- Add cranberries and boil it. Lower the heat and boil for 15 minutes.
- Add orange zest and boil for a few minutes.
- Pour the cranberry sauce into hot jars.
- Remove air bubbles and wipe the rim.
- Place the jar in a boiling water canner. Process for 15 minutes.
- Turn off the heat, remove the lid, and let the jars stand for 5 minutes. Remove jars and cool for 12-24 hours. Check lids for seal; they should not flex when the center is pressed.

NUTRITION

Calories 103, Protein 0g,
Carbohydrate 27g, Fat 0g,
Sugar 24g

TOMATO CHUTNEY

Prep time: 30 min
Cook time: 2 hrs

Serving: 6 jars

INGREDIENTS:

- 4 lbs tomatoes, peeled, cored and chopped
- 1 cup onions, chopped
- ¼ cup garlic, minced
- ½ cup raisins, chopped
- ¾ cup brown sugar
- ¾ cup white sugar
- 1 ½ cups apple cider vinegar
- 1 tbsp pickling salt
- 1 lime, zested and juiced
- 1 tbsp ground ginger
- 1-3 tbsp hot pepper flakes
- ½ tsp ground cumin
- ½ tsp black pepper

DIRECTIONS:

- Transfer the core and quarter tomatoes to the food processor and pulse until smooth.
- Add tomatoes and remaining ingredients to the pot and boil over high heat. Then, lower the heat and cook at low simmer for 1 ½ to 2 hours.
- Prepare the water bath canner.
- Ladle the chutney to the canning jar and seal it.
- Transfer the canning jar to the water bath canner. Boil for 10 minutes.
- When done, turn off heat. Remove lid and let jars sit for 5 minutes.
- Then, check seals and store it in a dark and cool place.

NUTRITION

Calories 42, Protein 1g, Carbohydrate 10g, Fat 1g, Sugar 8g

RHUBARB CHUTNEY

Prep time: 45 min
Cook time: 45 min

Serving: 6 jars

INGREDIENTS:

- 2 ½ lbs rhubarb, trimmed and sliced thin
- 1 cup brown sugar
- ¾ cup honey
- 1 cup apple cider vinegar
- ½ cup onion, chopped
- 1 cup raisins, chopped
- 1 ½ tbsp ginger, grated
- 1 tsp ground cinnamon
- ½ tsp ground allspice
- 1 tsp sea salt
- 2 ½ tsp red pepper flakes

NUTRITION

Calories 54, Protein 1g,
Carbohydrate 14g, Fat 1g,
Sugar 10g

DIRECTIONS:

- Add all ingredients to the pot and stir well. Boil over high heat.
- Then, lower the heat and cook for 30 minutes.
- Prepare the water bath canner. Transfer the mixture to the jar and seal it. Place the jars to the water bath canner. Boil for 15 minutes.
- When done, remove the lid and let jars sit in the canner for 5 minutes.
- Check seals before labeling and storing in a cool, dark place. Refrigerate any jars that didn't seal to use within 3 to 4 weeks.

SWEETENED CHERRY CHUTNEY

Prep time: 1 hr
Cook time: 1 hr

Serving: 9 jars

INGREDIENTS:

- 4 lbs cherries, pitted and halved or chopped
- 1 ½ cups onion, chopped
- 1 ½ cups honey
- 1 ¾ cups apple cider vinegar
- 1 cup raisins, chopped
- 3 garlic, 3 cloves, minced
- 1 lime, zested and juiced
- 2 tbsp ginger, grated
- 1 tbsp dry mustard
- 2 tsp to 2 tbsp salt
- 2 tsp red pepper flakes

DIRECTIONS:

- Add all ingredients to the pot and boil it. Lower the heat and cook for 1 hour.
- When the chutney is cooking, prepare the canning jars and lids.
- Transfer the mixture to the canning jars.
- Prepare the water bath canner. Transfer the canning jar to the water bath canner. Boil for 15 minutes.
- Serve!

NUTRITION

Calories 27, Protein 1g,
Carbohydrate 19g, Fat 1g,
Sugar 16g

APPLE CHUTNEY

Prep time: 10 min
Cook time: 2 hrs 20 min

Serving: 9 jars

INGREDIENTS:

- 4 lbs apples, sliced, peeled
- 1 cup raisins
- 2 garlic cloves, minced
- ½ cup onion, chopped
- 5 oz preserved ginger, chopped
- 1 ½ tbsp chili powder
- 1 tbsp mustard seed
- 1 tsp curry powder
- 4 cups brown sugar
- 4 cups apple cider vinegar
- ¼ cup pickling spice

DIRECTIONS:

- Add all ingredients to the pot and stir well. Boil for 1 ½ hours.
- Transfer the mixture to the jar and place it in the water bath canner. Process for 15 minutes.
- Store it in the dark place.

NUTRITION

Calories 901, Protein 5g, Carbohydrate 223g, Fat 2g, Sugar 206g

PUMPKIN AND APRICOT CHUTNEY

Prep time: 5 min
Cook time: 1 hr

Serving: 4 jars

INGREDIENTS:

- 2 ½ cups pumpkin, peeled and diced
- 1 cup onion, chopped
- ½ chili, chopped
- 4 tbsp dried apricots, chopped
- 4 tbsp sultanas
- 2 cups brown sugar
- 1 tbsp ginger fresh ginger, grated
- 1 cup cider vinegar

DIRECTIONS:

- Add all ingredients to the pot and cook for 1 hour.
- Prepare the water bath canner. Transfer the mixture to the jar.
- Process for 15 minutes.
- When done, remove the jars from the canner.
- Allow it to sit for 5 minutes.
- Store it in a dark place.

NUTRITION

Calories 317, Protein 3g,
Carbohydrate 79g, Fat 1g,
Sugar 68g

Grab Your Own Canning Kit
at
www.HillHjem.com

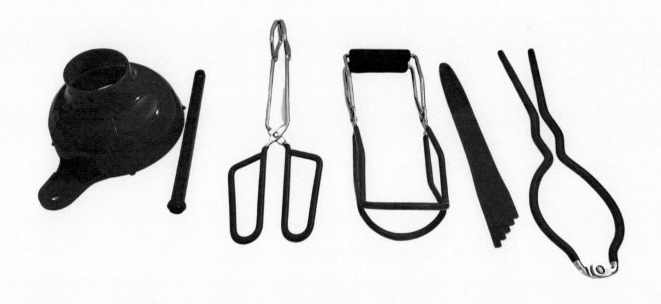

Also on Amazon!

Thank you for supporting our small family business!

Learn more at:

www.HillHjem.com

Made in the USA
Columbia, SC
12 August 2024